Second Edition

Economical
Writing

Second Edition

Economical
Writing

Deirdre N. McCloskey

University of Iowa
and
Erasmus University of Rotterdam

WAVELAND
PRESS, INC.
Long Grove, Illinois

For information about this book, contact:
Waveland Press, Inc.
4180 IL Route 83, Suite 101
Long Grove, IL 60047-9580
(847) 634-0081
info@waveland.com
www.waveland.com

10-digit ISBN 1-57766-063-3
13-digit ISBN 978-1-57766-063-7

Printed in the United States of America

20   19   18   17   16

Books by Deirdre McCloskey

Contents

Preface

The implied reader of my little book is a student of economics or of related fields who needs to write. The book originated in a course for graduate economics students at the University of Chicago in the 1970s. I thank the students for their help. An earlier version, directed at young teachers of economics, appeared under the present title in the April 1985 issue of *Economic Inquiry*, and something very like the present edition appeared in book form at Macmillan of New York in 1987 as *The Writing of Economics*, long out of print.

I thank a group of good writers who have improved the argument by telling me where it was wrong or right: Eleanor Birch, Thomas Borcherding, Ross Echert, Clifford Geertz, Albert Hirschman, Sara Hirschman, Linda Kerber, Charles Kindleberger, Meir Kohn, David Landes, much of the McCloskey family (Laura, Helen, and Joanne), Joel Mokyr, Erin Newton, Carol Rowe, much of the Solow family (John, Barbara, and Robert), Richard Sutch, the late Donald Sutherland, Steven Webb, A. Wick, and Barbara Yerkes. Getting someone to criticize a piece of writing early is a good practice, though students seldom have time to follow it. Better to be criticized harshly by friends in private, and fix what is wrong, than to be massacred in public. I've had the benefit.

In publishing the first edition Anthony English, then at Macmillan, was his usual tasteful and energetic self. Tony was the last editor of the little book by Strunk and White, and it flattered me to see my own *libellus* in the same form. Cathy Hansen gave it a good student's-eye reading in the old edition. My assistant Deborah Reese got me a word processed version to work on. Marguerite Knoedel, who typed the many drafts before the days of word processing, knows that I'm not joking when I say that even passable writing involves rewriting again and again and again. Hemingway rewrote the last page of *Farewell to Arms* sixty times. Sixty. In pencil. The John Simon Guggenheim Foundation, the National Endowment for the Humanities, the Institute for Advanced Study, and the University of Iowa gave me the time.

Why You Should Not
Stop Reading Here

The man in the street loves his mistaken opinions about free trade, and will not listen to professors of economics. His opinions are his own, after all, and free trade is "just a matter of opinion." Everyone is "entitled to his opinion in a free country." Phooey to the professors.

But as a student of economics you have read the chapter on comparative advantage in your Ec 1 text and you know that the man in the street is wrong. It's like that with writing. Most writers have at first the man in the street's attitude toward what they write. They don't know the rules. They won't look into professional advice on writing. They never rewrite. They can't read the page they wrote yesterday with a cold eye. They admire uncritically everything they've written, favoring their mistakes as God-given and personal. Just matters of opinion.

Now it's true that you can't change your character traits, very much, and it's offensive for some louse to criticize them:

Linus: What's this?

Lucy: This is something to help you be a better person next year. . . . This is a list I made up of *all* your faults. [Exit]

Linus [reading, increasingly indignant]: Faults? You call these *faults*? These aren't faults! These are *character traits*!

Amateur writers suppose that writing is a character trait instead of a skill. If someone says that it's clumsy to use "not only. . . but also" or that it's phony to use "prioritize" they

1

are liable to react the way they react to remarks about their body shape. Hey, that's who I am; lay off, you louse. The professionals, by contrast, such as poets and journalists and the best writers of economics, have learned to take advantage of criticism.

The first and the biggest truth about writing is that we all—you, I, and Dave Barry—can use more criticism. We would be a lot more professional if we took more of it.

1
Writing Is the Economist's Trade

In a "Shoe" strip the uncle bird comes in the front door with a briefcase overflowing with paper and says to the nephew bird, "I'm exhausted, but I've got to work: I've got to get this report out by tomorrow morning." Next panel: "I'll be up until 3:00 writing it." Last panel, picturing the nephew with a horrified look on his face: "You mean homework is *forever*?!" Yes, dear, homework is forever. A lot of it is writing.

Non-economists have been complaining about economic and other social scientific writing for quite a while (Williamson 1947). Older economists mainly shrug off their responsibility to teach the young to write, offering the strange excuse that the young won't pay attention. (You'll remember that your lack of attention didn't stop them from explaining income and substitution effects in three different ways.) Only a few economists have written about economic writing. Walter Salant did his part in an essay published in 1969. J. K. Galbraith wrote a piece called "Writing, Typing and Economics." He was using Hemingway's crack about a bad writer: "That's not writing: that's typing." A lot of economics isn't even very good typing.

The lack of interest in economical writing doesn't come from a lack of importance. But no one tells the beginner in a trade with a lot of writing how important it is to learn the skill. The researchers at the Department of Agriculture care about writing; so do Federal Reserve banks; private companies do a lot of business by writing. And of course professors of economics must write. The big secret in economics is that good writing pays well and bad writing pays badly. Honest. Rotten writing causes more papers and reports to fail than do rotten statistics or rotten research. You have to be read to be listened to. Bad writing is not read, even by professors or bosses paid to read it. Can you imagine actually *reading* the worst term paper you've ever turned in? Your sainted mother herself wouldn't.

Economics teaches things slightly off the point. The courses don't tell you directly how to do economics—they tell you *about* it, but not how to do it—and most programs offer little in the way of on-the-job practice. Students are taught minor details in statistics when the hard business of quantitative thinking in economics is getting the data straight; they are taught minor details in mathematics when the hard business of mathematical economics is getting economic ideas straight. (In fact they are often taught *mistaken* details: that statistical significance, for example, has anything to do with substantive significance; or that a proof on a blackboard is the same thing as a proof in the world [McCloskey 1998; McCloskey and Ziliak 1996]). In most schools they are taught nothing about writing, when the hard business of economic thinking is getting the words straight. The master carpenter turns her back on the apprentice, concealing the tricks of the trade, such as cutting a board clean.

The reason for learning to cut it clean, I repeat, is that the skill is used a lot. What economists do, and what people educated in economics do even if they never see a demand curve after their education, depends on writing, because writing is the cheapest way to reach a big audience, especially in the age of the Internet, and because writing forces the writer to think. An economically trained person is likely to spend most of her working life writing papers, reports, memoranda, proposals, columns, and letters. Economics depends much more on writing (and on speaking, another neglected art) than on the statistics and mathematics usually touted as the tools of the trade. Most of the economist's skills are verbal. An economist should be embarrassed to do such a large part of the craft unprofessionally. Shame on us.

2
Writing Is Thinking

The usual reply is, "That's just a matter of style: after all, it's content that matters." Students will sometimes complain about bad grades earned for writing badly, arguing that they had the *content* right, or that they *meant* to say the right thing (people who are complaining about grades speak in *italics*).

Now the influence of mere style is greater than you think. The history of ideas has many wide turns caused by "mere" lucidity and elegance of expression. Galileo's *Dialogo* of 1632 persuaded people that the earth went around the sun, but not because it was a Copernican tract (there were others) or because it contained much new evidence (it did not). It was persuasive because it was a masterpiece of Italian prose. Poincaré's good French and Einstein's good German early in this century were no small contributors to their influence on mathematics and physics. John Maynard Keynes (rhymes with "brains") hypnotized three generations of economists and politicians with his graceful fluency in English. Keynes is acknowledged as the best writer that economics has had. (See, however, the hostile dissection of the style of a passage from Keynes in Graves and Hodge [1943 (1961), pp. 332–340]. It makes one wince, that our best is so easy to fault.)

But the real problem is the premise that you can split content from style. It's wrong. They are yolk and white in a scrambled egg. Economically speaking, the production function for thinking cannot be written as the sum of two subfunctions, one producing "results" and the other "writing them up." The function is not separable. You do not learn the details of an argument until writing it in detail, and in writing the details you uncover flaws in the fundamentals. Thinking requires detail: you can't add 21 and 27 if you get all fuzzy about whether 2 plus 2 equals 4 or 5. You have to know for sure. Good thinking is accurate, symmetrical, relevant to the thoughts of the audience, concrete yet usefully abstract, concise yet usefully full; above all it is self-critical and honest. So too is good writing.

Good writers in economics write self-critically and honestly, trying to say what they mean. They sometimes discover in the act of writing that what looked persuasive when floating vaguely in the mind looks foolish when moored to the page. Better, they discover truths they didn't know they had. They refine their fuzzy notion of an obstacle to trade by finding the right word to describe it; they see the other side of a market by writing about the demand side with clarity. Annie Dillard says in *The Writing Life*,

> When you write, you lay out a line of words. The line of words is a miner's pick, a woodcarver's gouge, a surgeon's probe. You wield it, and it digs a path you follow. Soon you find yourself deep in new territory. . . . The writing has changed, in your hands, and in a twinkling, from an expression of your notions to an epistemological tool. (Dillard 1989, p. 3)

Writing resembles mathematics. Mathematics is a language, an instrument of communication. But so too language is a mathematics, an instrument of thought.

3
Rules Can Help, But Bad Rules Hurt

Like mathematics, writing can be learned. It's an evasion to talk of writing as a natural gift, a free lunch from the gods, which some people have and some just don't. Although we can't all become Mark Twains or George Orwells, anyone can write better. In fact Twain and Orwell worked at explaining how (Twain 1895; Orwell 1946).

Elementary writing can be learned like high school algebra. On the simplest level neither is inborn. Only a few people can prove important new theorems in mathematics, about as few as can write regularly for the *New Yorker*. Yet anyone can learn to solve a set of simultaneous equations, just as anyone can learn to delete a quarter of the words from a first draft. Like mathematics at the simplest level, good writing at the simplest level follows rules.

There are scores of rulebooks on writing, most of them pretty good (by the way, the computer programs that claim to help you with writing are useless; maybe someday they will get better, but right now they are terrible, written by people who don't know how). You can find the good rulebooks in the writing section of any big bookstore. My three favorites, from elementary to advanced, are William Strunk, Jr. and E. B. White, *The Elements of Style* (1959 and later editions); Robert Graves and Alan Hodge, *The Reader Over Your Shoulder: A Handbook for Writers of English Prose* (1943 and later editions); and Joseph M. Williams, *Style: Toward Clarity and Grace* (1981; 5th ed. 1996). Not everyone will get as much as I did from these three, but Strunk and White is fundamental: you can't be any kind of professional writer if you haven't read and taken to heart its little lessons. Other texts I know and admire are Richard A. Lanham, *Revising Prose* (1979; 3rd ed. 1992) and his *Revising Business Prose* (3rd ed. 1992); and Wayne Booth, Gregory Colomb, and Joseph Williams, *The Craft of Research* (1995). Some more advanced books are F. L. Lucas, *Style* (1955); Jacques Barzun, *Simple and Direct: A Rhetoric for Writers* (1976; revised ed. 1994); part III of Jacques Barzun and Henry F. Graff, *The Modern Researcher* (1970); Paul R. Halmos, pp. 19–48 in Norman E. Steenrod et al., *How to Write Mathematics* (1973; 2nd ed. 1981); Sir Ernest Gowers, *The Complete Plain Words* (1962 and subsequent editions); Howard S. Becker, *Writing for Social Scientists* (1986); William E. Blundell, *The Art and Craft of Feature Writing* (1980, by a writer for the *Wall Street Journal*); Francis-Noel Thomas and Mark Turner, *Clear and Simple as the Truth: Writing Classic Prose* (1994); and anything by Annie Dillard, such as *The Writing Life* (1989).

The rules I give here, many of them the same as the other books give, will be depressing at first, because of their great number ("Number 613: Query any sentence with more than two adjectives in it") and their vagueness ("Be clear"—but, you ask, how?). What you are really trying to learn is like good sewing or carpentry, watching what you're doing and giving it some thought. If you resolve right now to put away your amateur attitude toward writing and to start watching and thinking, you'll do fine in the end. Meanwhile, just like the first steps in sewing or carpentry, there are rules and rules and more rules.

Don't believe everyone, though, who sets up as a teacher of the rules. The first rule is that many of the rules we learned in Miss Jones' class in the eighth grade are wrong. Sometimes of course Miss Jones had a point. For example, dangling out on a limb alone, she justly castigated participles badly placed in a sentence. Her strictures against "I" make no sense if they merely result in replacing "I" with "we," but do make sense if you see that when you're talking about "I" (or "we") you're not talking about the subject. Yet in other ways her list of rules and the folk wisdom that reinforced it have done damage.

"Never repeat the same word or phrase within three lines," said Miss Jones, and because the rule fit splendidly with our budding verbosity at age 13 we adopted it as the habit of a lifetime. Now we can't mention the "consumer" in one line without an itch to call it the "household" in the next and the "agent" in the next. Our readers slip into a fog known in the writing trade as "elegant variation."

"Never write 'I'," wrote she, and we (and you and I) have drowned in "we" ever since, a "we" less suited to mere economists than to kings, editors, and people with tapeworms.

"Don't be common; emulate James Fenimore Cooper; writing well is writing swell," said she, praising Harry Whimple and his fancy talk—and in later life we struggled to attain a splendidly dignified bureaucratese.

Miss Jones ruled against our urge to freely split infinitives. H. W. Fowler, who wrote in 1926 an amusing book on the unpromising subject of *Modern English Usage*, knew how to handle her (1926 [1965], article "Split Infinitives"): "Those who neither know nor care [what a split infinitive is] are the vast majority, and are a happy folk, to be envied by most. . . . 'To really understand' comes readier to their lips and pens than 'really to understand'; they see no reason why they should not say it (small blame to them, seeing that reasons are not their critics' strong point)."

Miss Jones filled us with guilt about using a preposition to end a sentence with. Winston Churchill, a politician of note who wrote English well, knew how to handle her and the editor who meddled with his preposition-ended sentence. He wrote in the margin of his manuscript corrected by a student of Miss Jones, "This is the sort of impertinence up with which I will not put."

Worst of all, Miss Jones fastened onto our impressionable minds the terrible, iterative rule of Jonesian arrangement: "Say what you're going to say; say it; say that you've said it." The Jonesian rule has nearly ruined economic prose. Papers in economics consist mostly of summary, outline, anticipation, announcement, redundancy, and review. They never get to the point.

4

Be Thou Clear; But for Lord's Sake Have Fun, Too

The one genuine rule, a golden one, is Be Clear. A Roman professor of writing and speaking put it this way: "Therefore one ought to take care to write not merely so that the reader *can* understand but so that he cannot possibly *misunderstand*" (Quintilian, Book VIII, ii, 24). Clarity is a social matter, not something to be decided unilaterally by the writer. The reader like the consumer is sovereign. *If the reader thinks what you write is unclear, then it is, by definition.* Quit arguing. Karl Popper, a philosopher with a good style and a correspondingly wide influence, wrote: "I learned never to defend anything I had written against the accusation that it is not clear enough. If a conscientious reader finds a passage unclear, it has to be re-written. . . . I write, as it were, with somebody constantly looking over my shoulder and constantly pointing out to me passages that are not clear" (p. 83).

Clarity is a matter of speed directed at the point. Bad writing stops you with a puzzle in every other sentence. It sends you off in irrelevant directions. It distracts you from the point, provoking irritated questions about what the subject is now, what the connection might be with the subject a moment ago, and why the words differ. You are always losing your way. Bad writing makes slow reading. The practice of Graves and Hodge in compiling the bad examples for their principles of clear and graceful expression was "to glance at every book or paper we found lying about and, whenever our reading pace was checked by some difficulty of expression, to note the cause" (p. 127). (Their own sentence, incidentally, illustrates one rule of reading pace they could have followed better: Do Not Overuse Commas.)

In most writing the reader is in trouble more than half the time. You can see this by watching your own troubles. Notice in the present long and involved sentence, since there is a lot of clumsy intrusion of brand new stuff and the jumps in elevation of lingo, how no one could follow it, at least on first reading without having to go over it two, three times, because it is ungrammatical, which means not only that it breaks a Miss Jones Rule but also that it confuses you and anyone else, a reader, who happens to be reading, by violating your expectations, and that it has too much in it anyway, with no pleasing arrangement, which would make sense of it. You stumble and yawn and wander when you read such stuff.

Reading your own writing cold, a week after drafting it, will show you places where even you can*not* follow the sense with ease. Knock such places into shape. If the readers have too much trouble they give up. Lack of clarity is selfish and confusing. The writer is wasting your time. Up with this you need not put.

Telling someone who is not already an accomplished writer to "Be Clear," though, is not a lot of help. It has been said that "It is as hard to write well as to be good." In the abstract the golden rule of writing clearly helps about as much as the golden rule of other doings, of which it is a corollary. "All things whatsoever ye would that men should do to you, do ye even so to them." Well, sure, yes, all right; but how?

And wait a minute. All this talk of "rules"—which the rest of the book is going to continue—sounds awfully grim. It is, and necessarily so. But once you learn a few of the rules and start applying them you'll start to be able to play the Game of Writing. It's not just grim following of rules, a death march to the Department of English. It's great fun to get a sentence just right, in the same way that it's fun to get a dish you're cooking just right or a double play in softball just right. The psychologist Mihaly Csikszentmihalyi ("CHICK-sent-mee-high-ee") has discovered that happiness is not a six-pack and a sport utility vehicle but what he calls "flow," which occurs "when a person's skills are fully involved in overcoming a challenge that is just about manageable" (1997, p. 30). Flow makes work into play and play into work. The rhetorician Richard Lanham argues that the best way to teach yourself writing is to indulge in a certain amount of clowning in prose. You take words seriously by playing with them, overcoming an artistic challenge that is just about manageable.

Back to the rules—though I hope you see from my style that I don't think life should be mainly rule driven. Learn the rules in order to have fun. To have a fulfilled life you want to achieve flow. Believe me, skillful writing is one way.

5
The Rules Are Factual
Rather Than Logical

The rules come from observation. In the best writing, you do not stumble. It's no trick to spot a bad sentence and to see what went wrong. Just read. You feel it, like rain or sunshine. You know that George Orwell wrote well, that Mary McCarthy doesn't take many false steps, that you seldom have difficulty understanding what Tom Wolfe is talking about. Dr. Johnson said two centuries ago: He who would acquire a good style should devote his days and nights to the study of Joseph Addison. Well, likewise: Orwell, McCarthy, and Wolfe.

In recent economics the list would include Akerlof, Arrow, Boulding, Bronfenbrenner, Buchanan, Caves, Easterlin, Fogel, Frank, Friedman, Haberler, Harberger, Heilbroner, Hirschman, Hughes, Galbraith, Gerschenkron, Griliches, Harry Johnson, Keynes, Kindleberger, Lebergott, Leijonhufvud, Olson, Robertson, Joan Robinson, Rostow, Schelling, Schumpeter, Theodore Schultz, Solow, Stigler, Tobin, Tullock, and Yeager. Pay attention to how they write: this is as good as it gets. The diminishing returns in the list are sharp. Even economists who take some pains with their style will overuse "we," the passive voice, and fancy talk from Latin and Greek ("We perceive that equilibrium is achieved by a process of successive approximations").

You can't define good style without a list of good writers. (A list compiled statistically by the economist Arthur Diamond showed that the best writer in economics was, uh, . . . me, Deirdre McCloskey. Depressing news. I *know* how badly I write. If I'm the best . . .). Good style is what good writers do. Double negatives, for example, aren't "illogical" (modern French and ancient Greek have them); they are social mistakes, at least right now. If Orwell and his kind start using "I ain't no fool," no amount of schoolmaster logic can stand in the way of its imitation. In matters of taste the only standard is the practice of good people. Furthermore, everything from the standard of proof in number theory to the standard of skill in baton twirling is a matter of taste. You find out who is good by comparing good with bad.

A reader grades writers by stylistic competence. The violation of the rules of clarity and grace sends a signal of incompetence. If you start sentences habitually with "However" the reader will discover that you are an incompetent writer in other ways, too. Because the violations signal incompetence they are correlated with each other. It's a good bet that a writer who doesn't know how to express parallel ideas in parallel form, and doesn't care, will also not know how to avoid excessive summarization and anticipation. It's about as good a bet that she will not know how to think, and will not care.

6
Classical Rhetoric Guides Even the Economical Writer

Essays are made from bunches of paragraphs, which are made from bunches of sentences, which are made from bunches of words. Before you start an essay choose a subject that meets the assignment yet stirs something in your soul (you cannot work on a subject unless you love it or hate it; you should therefore do your economic history on the fashion industry and your industrial organization on advertising). The rules about whole essays or paragraphs are most useful at the stage of first composition; the rules about sentences and words at the stage of final revision. Some rules apply everywhere: it is good to be brief in the whole essay and in the single word, during the midnight fever of composition and the morning chill of revision. Brevity is the soul of clarity, too. Yet the rules of writing can be stuffed if necessary into boxes by diminishing size from essay to word.

What is needed for this is an economic rhetoric. I do not mean by "rhetoric" a frill, or a device for lying—the politician's "heated rhetoric" at a news conference or the professor's "bad rhetoric" when arguing a weak case. I mean the whole art of argument, which is its classical and correct meaning. It is the art, as Wayne Booth put it (1974, p. 59), "of discovering warrantable beliefs and improving those beliefs in shared discourse."

The three important parts of classical rhetoric were invention, arrangement, and style. Invention, the framing of arguments worth listening to, is the business of economic theory and of empirical economics. Theory and empirical economics have been hurt by an official methodology which an awareness of rhetoric can heal (McCloskey 1998). It helps to see, for instance, that some economic arguments are a series of analogies. Saying that the market for automobiles is "just like" a diagram of demand and supply is, when you think about it, bizarre. Not false: bizarre. It is also bizarre to compare a beloved to a summer's day, but Shakespeare did it, exploring its persuasiveness. Economic models are economic poetry.

The economic poems make remarks about each other, as poems do. Once you have solved one problem by stating it as an analogy you can use the problem as an analogy for others. Suppose you come to understand that a waitress who customarily gets tips is not necessarily better off because of the custom: without tipping she would have to get a higher salary to retain her and others in the industry. The analogy here is of waitresses to business tycoons or gold dealers. Once you have grasped the primary analogy you can see others later as analogies to it. Someone says, "Safety regulations help coal miners." You think: "Ah, hah! That's just the Tipped Waitress Problem," and then say out loud, astonishing your audience with your economic brilliance, "No, without the safety regulations they would be paid more: so only the miners who value health highly compared to money are better off." You have used analogy, part of the rhetoric of economics. It's the main way that economists approach the getting of ideas.

Arrangement, too, is a part of economic rhetoric not much examined. A good deal of economic prose implies that the only proper arrangement of an empirical essay is introduction, outline of the rest of the paper, theory, (linear) model, results, suggestions for future research (since nothing ever works), and (again) summary. One rarely sees experiments with alternative arrangements, such as dialogues or reports on the actual sequence of the author's discovery. At any rate one does not see them in print. When economists talk among themselves, in the seminar room or hallway, the dialogue is the whole point, usually introduced by a report in sequence of "how I actually came to this subject." Economists might try learning good arrangement from their own behavior.

An official arrangement has spread to the social sciences from physics and biology. It is supposed to make social sciences more scientific to have a section entitled "Data" or "Results." The official rhetoric is a poor one. It does not tell what needs to be known—which experiments failed, what mathematics proved fruitless, why exactly the questions were asked in the way they were (see Medawar, 1964). It's better to make your own outline, one that fits your argument.

7
Fluency Can Be Achieved by Grit

The third branch of classical rhetoric, style, is easier to teach. It begins with mere fluency, getting the stuff down on paper. And it ends with revising again and again, until you've removed all the traps and ugliness.

You will have done some research (this is known as "thinking" and "reading" and "calculating") and are sitting down to write. Sitting down to write can be a problem, for it is then that your subconscious, which is dismayed by the anxiety of filling up blank pieces of paper, suggests that it would be ever so much more fun to do the dishes or to go get the mail. Sneak up on it and surprise it with the ancient recipe for success in intellectual pursuits: locate chair; apply rear end to it; locate writing implement; use it. You may wish to increase the element of surprise by writing standing at a tall desk, as my colleague Gary Fethke does. Once at the desk, though, you will find your subconscious drawing on various reserves of strength to persuade you to stop: fear, boredom, the impulse to track down that trivial point by adjourning to the library. Time to go see Mary or John. Time to watch the basketball game. Time to get some fresh air. Don't. Resist. It's time to write.

One of these distractions is taste. The trouble with developing good taste in writing, which is the point of studying books like this one, is that you begin to find your stuff distasteful. This creates doubt. Waves of doubt—the conviction that everything you've done so far is rubbish—will wash over you from time to time. The only help is a cheerful faith that more work will raise even this rubbish up to your newly acquired standards. Once achieved, you can reraise the standards and acquire better doubt at a level of still better taste. Buck up. Irrational cheerfulness is hard to teach but good to have for any work.

8
Write Early Rather Than Late

The teachable trick is getting a first draft. Don't wait until the research is done to begin writing because writing, to repeat, is a way of thinking. Be writing all the time, working on a page or two here, a section there. Research *is* writing. As a real student you will have notes, bits of prose to be placed in the mosaic. It often helps to give each note a title stating its gist, or at least a key word. Though any writing surface from clay tablet to computer screen can hold the notes, white 4" x 6" cards lined on one side are best when writing with a pen; with a word processor the best plan is just to spill out the notes as paragraphs, then print them out, cut them up with scissors, finding the best arrangement. Use one idea per card or per paragraph, even if the idea is only a single line. It's a mistake to economize by cramming several ideas into one space. Paper is cheap.

Manila folders are nice. In 1959 the American sociologist C. Wright Mills wrote an exhilarating essay, "On Intellectual Craftsmanship," in which he called the whole set of cards, folders, and so forth The File (which in computer talk has turned out to be virtually the same idea). "You must set up a file, which is, I suppose, a sociologist's way of saying: Keep a journal. Many creative writers keep journals; the sociologist's [and economist's] need for systematic reflection demands it" (p. 196). The file should become thick and rich, dumped out on the floor occasionally (or printed out and cut up) and rearranged.

Read through the file (which is invention) trying to see an outline in it (which is arrangement). The first outline will be broad. Allocate the cards or strips of printed and cut up paper to related stacks. Add notes reminding you of transitions and new ideas that occur to you as you ponder the file. Arrangement is like good statistical work, searching the data for patterns. It's like good dramatic work, too, searching the audience for response. Your arrangement should be artful. Make it interesting.

Now set aside the broad outline, keeping it steadily in mind. You need it as a goal to give the writing direction. You can change it, and should do so as the essay takes shape. Pick a little part of the outline to write about today. It need not be the beginning, though it's sometimes difficult to write first drafts any other way. The paper should be a story because readers normally read from beginning to end. Use the mad, creative file that is your brain. You need a certain intensity for all this. Writing cannot be done entirely as a routine, like peeling potatoes.

Write another outline if you get stuck (never stop for outlining if you're not stuck), a narrower one about the points you are going to write in the next few sentences or paragraphs, checking off the points as you write. Arrangement is a matter of finding good outlines, from the level of the book down to the level of the paragraph. The points in all outlines from broad to narrow should be substantive, not formal: not "Introduction" or "Concluding Paragraph" but "Economists pay no attention to the sexual division of labor" and "Housework should be included in national income"; or in a telegraphic style, "div. lab." and "housewk & GDP." Keep a piece of paper at hand to try out turns of phrase or to note ideas that occur in advance of their use.

When you get an inspiration, do not depend on your memory to keep it. A phrase or word will jog it. Don't let the moment pass.

9
You Will Need Tools

You will need an outline sitting on your desk, covered with notes for revision, some scratch paper for trying out things, and your file up on your screen. Don't worry about being neat: clean up in a dull moment.

You will need certain other bits of capital in abundance. Word processing devices are convenient and relatively inexpensive. You should find pleasure in exercising the tools of writing. An expensive and well balanced fountain pen is old-fashioned, but fun to use when the mood strikes. Indulge yourself. On the other hand, try not to become compulsive about equipment and procedures and surroundings. Ernest Hemingway used to sharpen forty pencils with a jackknife before beginning to write. So he didn't write much, though a lot of it was good. Be more flexible than he was if you can manage it. Look on yourself as an honest-to-goodness professional writer (which is what you are) who can do any job on command anywhere with any equipment whatever, Ernie Pyle pecking out dispatches on a portable typewriter from a foxhole on the Italian front in 1944.

Most people compose these days at a computer screen, some use dictatation software, and some old fogies whom I love dearly still write out everything in longhand on big yellow legal pads. A new medium will change your style, perhaps for the better. Switching from medium to medium is worth trying, because each medium suggests new arrangements. Here's an odd but valuable tip: if you change the typeface on your draft you will see it in a new light. As Richard Lanham, a master of these things, advised, "toggle."

The next most important tool is a dictionary. Every place you read or write should have its own dictionary. Do not use the crummy little paperback dictionaries: they do not lie flat and therefore require two hands to use. Use the big college dictionaries. Buy them secondhand for a few bucks and then scatter them around your apartment (being up-to-date is unimportant in a dictionary except for some details of spelling, like hyphenation). A good one is *Webster's New World Dictionary of the American Language*. It's handsomely produced, does a good job at word origins, notes Americanisms (handy when writing to non-Americans), gives easy-to-follow pronunciation guides (handy when speaking), and distinguishes levels of usage. Only if your computer software has an exceptionally good dictionary and you can access it quicker than you can reach over and look up the word can you do without the book.

A dictionary is more than a spelling list. Pause to read the definitions and the word origins. Part of the purpose again is to write well in the sense of not making embarrassing mistakes in usage. If you think "disinterested" means the same thing as "uninterested," for instance, you need to get acquainted with a dictionary and to start reading good writing with it at hand. Yet beyond what is meet and proper (look up "meet," noting that in this sense it is related to "medical"), wordlore will make you grow as a wordsmith. Learn to like words and to inquire about their backgrounds. It's a useful friendship, a joy of life.

English spelling would drive anybody nuts. The playwright George Bernard Shaw noted once that you could spell the word "fish" in English as "ghoti" (gh as in enou*gh*, o as in women, and ti as in nation). It's astonishing that anyone learns to spell according to Webster. In the sixteenth century nobody much cared, and Shakespeare (Shakspere, Shakespere) spelt 'em as hee plees'd. But nowadays you must spell according to Webster or you look like a careless dolt. It's stupid and unfair but that's the way things are. Students chronically misspell a few words, such as "receive" (remember: i before e except after c; but what about "leisure," "either," "weird," or for that matter "Deirdre"?); "separate" (pronounce the verb form carefully—"*sepa*-RATE"—and you'll remember it); schedule (which I could not spell until graduate school); whether (as against rain and shine); their (as against over there or where they're).

The spellchecker is a great innovation: for Lord's sake use it. Never turn in anything to anyone, and certainly not to a teacher or boss whose opinion matters if you haven't spellchecked. (Though remember that you have to choose "their" and "there" and "they're" for yourself; and hundreds of other choices; no substitute for giving the paper that last, slow rereading.)

A thesaurus (Greek: "treasure") shows you the precise word within a more or less fuzzy region of the language. Use a big one, not the pocket versions. Unfortunately the so-called "thesaurus" available with most word processing programs is almost useless, because the choices are too small. The best thesaurus is *Roget's International Thesaurus*. I favor the old 3rd edition over later ones, which for some reason they decided to spoil. "Proper words in proper places, make the true definition of a style," said Jonathan Swift (the comma in the odd place is an eighteenth-century weirdness).

Dictionaries of quotations (Bartlett's, Oxford, Penguin) are worth having—not to extract ornamental remarks in the manner of the speaker at the Kiwanis Club (avoid quotation books organized by topic: you want them by author), but to find the precise words within a more or less fuzzy memory: What exactly did Swift say, weird comma and all?

It's instructive to keep a personal book of quotations, containing economic ideas you think are expressed well. It's called a "commonplace book," not because it's cheesy but because in classical rhetoric the commonly shared materials of invention were called *loci communes*, literally "the common places," or "usual topics," "*koinoi topoi*" in Greek. Well kept, such a book can be the writer's journal of which Mills spoke. Simon James published his for economics, as *A Dictionary of Economic Quotations* (1984), mainly British, which contains much encouraging evidence that British economists know how to turn a phrase.

10
Keep Your Spirits Up, Forge Ahead

Now start writing. Here I must become less helpful, not because I have been instructed to hold back the secrets of the trade but because creativity is scarce. Where exactly the next sentence comes from is not obvious. If it were obvious then novels and economics papers could be written by machine.

If you can't think of anything to say, you might well read more, calculate more, and in general research more. Most research, however, turns out to be irrelevant to the paper you finally write, which is another reason to mix writing with the researching. The writing forces you to ask questions about the facts that are strictly relevant. The next sentence will sometimes reveal that you didn't do all the right research. The guiding question in research (research is not the subject here, but I'm not charging extra) is So What? Answer that question in every sentence, and you will become a great scholar, or a millionaire; answer it once or twice in a ten-page paper, and you'll write a good one.

If after all this, though, you still have nothing to say, then perhaps your mind is poorly stocked with ideas in general. The solution is straightforward. Educate yourself. That is, live a life of wide experience, and spend big chunks of it reading the best our civilization has to offer. Begin tonight. It's not too late to join the great conversation:

> As civilized human beings, we are the inheritors, neither of an inquiry about ourselves and the world, nor of an accumu-

lating body of information, but of a conversation begun in the primeval forest and extended and made more articulate in the course of centuries. . . . Education, properly speaking, is an initiation . . . in which we acquire the intellectual and moral habits appropriate to conversation. (Oakeshott 1933, pp. 198–199)

Anyway, say it. Saying it out loud will help. If people wrote more the way they spoke, their writing would have more vigor (if they spoke more the way they wrote their speaking would have more precision). Writing expresses personality, as does the speaking voice: it is said that to write well you need merely to make yourself good and then write naturally. We are good when speaking to Mom or to a friend, and we write well to them.

You hear a sentence when you read it out loud. It's a good rule not to write anything you would be embarrassed to say to the intended audience. In tutorials at Oxford and Cambridge you have to read your writing out loud, and are embarrassed if it's stupid. That's why British people of a certain class and generation did not write stupidities. Don't write entirely silently, or you will write entirely stiffly. Good modern prose has the rhythms of actual speech—intelligent and honest actual speech, not the empty chatter of the sophomore trying to make it at the fraternity party or the waffling obscurity of the Labor Department bureaucrat trying to tell a lie about black teenage unemployment. We exaggerate the power of words to conceal a shameful intent. Generally the words expose it.

Regard the outline as an aid, not a master. When you get stuck, as you will, look at the outline, revise it, reread what you have written, reread the last bit out loud, talk to yourself about where it is going, imagine explaining it to a friend, try to imitate some way of speaking that Dennis or Maynard had, write a sentence parallel to the one just written, fill out the idea.

Don't panic if the words don't come easily. Try changing the surroundings. Move to the library, sharpen a pencil, visit the fridge, block out noise with earmuffs, put classical music in your stereo (Bach is best for thinking; I use Mozart; there's doubt concerning rap). Then get back to work. Don't expect to write easily all the time. Nobody does. Writing, like any form of thinking, flares and fizzles like a candle. Don't break off when on a burn. Don't let anyone entice you into watching a movie on TV; tell Jane to go away; resist breaking for a snack. Be selfish about your little candle of creation.

Keep the finished manuscript in some form handy for rereading and revising. This is not a problem with word processing, but you'll want to see the thing in hard copy, too. A loose-leaf ringbinder is good because it can be added to easily, is hard to misplace even on a crowded desk, and can be studied and revised while lying in bed.

When dull, and especially when starting a session, reread a chunk of the draft, pencil in hand, to insert, amend, revise, correct, cancel, delete, and improve. On a computer, scroll up a little and read what you've done as though you were a first-time reader, noting where your reading pace is checked by some difficulty of expression.

At the end of a session, or at any substantial break, *always write down your thoughts, however vague, on what will come next*. This is a very good tip. Don't get up without doing it, even to answer nature's call. Write or type the notes directly onto the end of the text, where they can be looked at and crossed off as used. A few scraps will do, and will save half an hour of warming up when you start again. Jean Piaget, a titan of psychology—not much of a stylist if one can judge from the English translations, but the matter here is fluency, not grace—remarked once (1980, p. 1), "It's better to stop in the middle of the sentence. Then you don't waste time starting up." Paul Halmos urged the mathematical writer to plan the next session at the end of the present one (1973, p. 28). After a session of writing, the ideas not yet used stand ready in the mind. Get them onto that ideal storage medium, the computer file.

11
Speak to an Audience of Human Beings

Style, to repeat, is rewriting, and rewriting can be learned in rules. Rewriting can be tiresome. The myth of the free lunch to the contrary, good or even adequate writing is easy for few writers, and some of the best writers work at it the hardest, to make less work for the reader. Hemingway said, "Easy writing makes hard reading." Balzac rewrote his novels from printer's proofs as often as 27 times, bankrupting himself with the expense (Lucas, p. 270). Virginia Woolf rewrote parts of *The Waves* twenty times. Writing really well takes as much devotion as playing an instrument really well. The great violinist Giardini was asked how long it took him to learn how to play: "Twelve hours a day for twenty years" (Lucas, p. 271). Yet in truth the practice hours are not as stressful as the performances. Once you are equipped with a technique for doing it well, much of the rewriting is pleasant and not excessively hard. Rewriting for style does not have the anxiety of invention and arrangement—that you will not be able to produce anything at all.

Look your audience directly in the eyes. Be honest with them. Ask who they are, aim the draft toward them, and keep hauling yourself back to facing them in revisions. Choose a reader and stick with her. Changing your implied reader is in an economic sense inefficient. There is no point in telling your reader in a paper on the oil industry that oil is a black, burnable fluid, then turning to an exposition that assumes the reader understands supply and demand curves.

If you've started with a pre-schooler for an implied reader you have to keep her around. Similarly, an article using the translog production function wastes motion if it rederives the elementary properties of a Cobb-Douglas production function. No one who has gotten so far into such an article will be innocent of Cobb-Douglas. The writing mixes up two mutually exclusive audiences.

Some find it best to choose an Implied Reader of imagination, an ideal economist; others find it best to choose a real person, such as Richard Sutch or good old Professor Smith or the friend down the hall. It is healthy discipline to be haunted by people with high standards (but with some sympathy for the enterprise) looking over your shoulder in imagination. It keeps the prose steady at one level of difficulty to imagine one master spirit. "How would Sutch see this?" If it embarrasses you, imagining how Sutch would read it, the stuff *is* embarrassing: fix it.

<u>12</u>
Avoid Boilerplate

Your writing must be interesting. This sounds harshly difficult. Few of us are great wits, and we know we aren't. But
you can avoid some dullnesses by rule. Choosing oneself as
the audience tends to dullness, since most of us admire
uncritically even dull products of our own brains. A reason-
ably correct recitation of the history of prices and interest
rates over the past ten years may strike its author as a
remarkable intellectual achievement, filled with drama and
novelty. But Richard Sutch, who knows it, or good old Professor Smith, who lived it, or the colleague down the hall
who couldn't care less about it, probably don't agree. Spare
them. Restatements of the well known bore the readers;
routine mathematical passages bore the readers; excessive
introduction and summarization bore the readers. Get to
the point that some skeptical but serious reader cares about
and stick to it.

Therefore, avoid boilerplate. Boilerplate in prose is all
that is prefabricated and predictable. It's common in economic prose. Excessive introduction and summarizing is
boilerplate; redoing for a large number of repetitive cases
what can be done just as well with a single well-chosen one
is boilerplate. The academic pose inspires boilerplate. Little
is getting accomplished with econometric chatter copied out
of the textbook, rederivations of the necessary conditions for
consumer equilibrium, and repetition of hackneyed formu-
lations of a theory.

Impenetrable theoretical utterances have prestige in economics. That's sad, because no scientific advance can be expected from such games on a blackboard. A young writer of economics will sacrifice any amount of relevance and clarity to show that she can play the game. The result is filigreed boilerplate. The economist will write about the completeness of arbitrage in this way: "Consider two cities, A and B, trading an asset, X. If the prices of X are the same in market A and in market B, then arbitrage may be said to be complete." The clear way does not draw attention to its "theoretical" character at all: "New York and London in 1870 both had markets for Union Pacific bonds. The question is, did the bonds sell for the same in both places?"

Never start a paper with that all-purpose filler for the bankrupt imagination, "This paper. . . ." Describing the art of writing book reviews, Jacques Barzun and Henry Graff note (p. 272) that "the opening statement takes the reader from where he presumably stands in point of knowledge and brings him to the book under review" (p. 272). In journalism it's called the "hook." A paper showing that monopoly greatly reduces income might best start: "Every economist knows by now that monopoly does not much reduce income [which is where he presumably stands in point of knowledge]. Every economist appears to be mistaken [thus bringing him to the matter under review]." It bores the reader to begin "*This paper* discusses the evidence for a large effect of monopoly on income." The reader's impulse, fully justified by the tiresome stuff to follow, is to give up.

Another piece of boilerplate, attached to the early parts of most student papers, is "background," a polite word for padding, the material you collected that you later discovered was beside the point. It seems a shame not to use it, you say; and after all it gives the thing weight. Resist. If you have read a lot and if you have been thinking through the question you began with, asking and answering one question after another, you will have plenty to say. If you haven't read a lot and did not think through the questions you are asking, you will have nothing to say. No one will be fooled: remember that professors and bosses are experts in detecting lack of effort and lack of success. You might as well spare a tree.

Still another piece of boilerplate, and one which kills the momentum of most papers in economics on the second page, is the table-of-contents paragraph: "The outline of this paper is as follows." Don't, please, please, for God's sake, don't. Nine out of ten readers skip to the substance, if they can find it. The few who pause on the paragraph are wasting their time. They can't understand the paragraph until, like the author, they have read the paper, at which point they don't need it. Usually the table-of-contents paragraph has been written with no particular audience in mind, least of all the audience of first-time readers of the paper. Even when done well it lacks a purpose. You will practically never see it in good writing, unless inserted by an editor who doesn't know good writing. Weak writers defend it as a "roadmap." They got the idea from Miss Jones: "Tell the reader what you're going to say. Say it. Say that you've said it." It's exceptionally bad advice, and the person who made up this memorable phrasing of it is burning right now in Hell.

Therefore, avoid overtures, and do not give elaborate summaries of what you have said. Never repeat without apologizing for it ("as I said earlier"; or merely "again"). Unless you apologize the reader thinks you have not noticed the repetition, and will suspect that you have not thought through the organization. She'll be right. Remember that the paper that took you days or a week to write will be read in about half an hour. You must read the paper yourself in this rapid way to get the experience the reader will have, and to make the experience good.

The writer who wishes to be readable does not clot his prose with traffic directions. He thinks hard about the arrangement. Add headings afterwards if you wish, especially ones with declarative sentences advancing the argument, like the ones used here. Your prose, however, should read well and clearly without the headings.

13
Control Your Tone

The tone of the writing and much of its clarity depends on choosing and then keeping an appropriate implied author, the character you pretend to be while writing: the Enthusiastic Student, the Earnest Scientist, the Reasonable and Modest Journeyman, the Genius, the Math Jock, the Professor, the Breezy Journalist. Look at a piece of economics and ask what Implied Author it has in mind. The successful piece will have an author the reader can tolerate. Writing is a little drama in which the writer chooses the roles. You cannot abstain as a writer from making a choice. You can't just "be yourself," though you will probably do a more persuasive job if the implied author in your writing is similar to yourself. Writing, like teaching or social life, is a performance, a job of acting.

Many times in your writing career, though, you will be required to be less than candid. It would be bad for a dean to tell everything in her memorandum—bad for the college, bad for the students. If you are the VP for Sales you are not under oath to reveal in your advertising that the competitor's product is better and cheaper. The ethical problem sits right in the middle of the road. "Rhetoric" gets a bad name from such problem cases—of having to tell less than the truth for another worthy goal. Being clear before you decide to hide the whole truth will at least make the choice plain. You won't be deciding to lie by accident. Welcome to life's dilemmas.

Everyone has a problem with tone—student and professor, employee and boss. The student will sometimes use an implied author encountered only in government forms, using phrases like "due to" and "period of time" and "views were opposing." No one really talks like this. Adopting the implied author The Newspaper Reporter is a natural alternative, since much of the reading a student does is from newspapers. The stuff will be snappy, but it's hard to tolerate outside the newspaper. The journalist writes for the one-paragraph jolt. A Hollywood autobiography ("with the assistance of Elmer Snerd") will have this implied author. It reads like a year's worth of the *National Enquirer.*

Out of stage fright, professors in economics overuse the pompous and unintelligible implied author The Scientist. Have pity on them, and help them overcome their fear. C. Wright Mills' discussion of the problem of writing sociology is applicable to economics and other academic writing:

> Such lack of ready intelligibility, I believe, usually has little or nothing to do with the complexity of subject matter, and nothing at all with profundity of thought. It has to do almost entirely with certain confusions of the academic writer about his own status. . . . [Because the academic writer in America] feels his own lack of public position, he often puts the claim for his own status before his claim for the attention of the reader to what he is saying. . . . Desire for status is one reason why academic men [and women: Mills lived in a notably sexist age] slip so readily into unintelligibility. . . . To overcome the academic *prose* you have first to overcome the academic *pose*. It is much less important to study grammar and Anglo-Saxon roots than to clarify your answer to these important questions: (1) How difficult and complex after all is my subject? (2) When I write, what status am I claiming for myself? (3) For whom am I trying to write? (p. 218 f.)

In other words, what spoils academic writing is lack of confidence.

It's really not that difficult to explain a Malthusian demographic model or a rational expectations model in plain words to smart people willing to pay attention. A reader of a student paper or of a professional journal is smart and willing. Above all, in other words, one must decide to be understood and worry some other time about being admired. Do not try to impress people who already understand the argument (they will not be amused). Try to explain it in a reasonable tone to people who do *not* now understand. Your roommate is a good choice of audience, or your professor: neither will stand still for fakery.

Tone of writing is like tone of voice. It is personality expressed in prose. Students would do better to reveal more of their character in their writing. A college teacher on the whole likes students (or else she would be selling insurance). So don't worry. Be nice, not servile or pompous. Similar words of comfort apply to the professor herself: relax; take off the mask of The Scientist; you're lovable.

The worst mistake is to be unpleasant: if you yell at people they will walk away, in reading as at a dorm party. Avoid invective. "This is pure nonsense"; "there is absolutely no evidence for this view"; "the hypothesis is fanciful" are fun phrases to write, deeply satisfying as only political and intellectual passion can be, but they arouse the suspicion in any but the most uncritical audience that the argument needs a tone of passion to overcome its weakness. Adam Smith (in his best book, *The Theory of Moral Sentiments*) pointed out that indignation by you the Author against That Idiot arouses in the reader sympathy for That

Idiot, which is not what your indignation was meant to achieve (I.ii.3.4).

Tone is transmitted by adverbs, those "-ly" words that drive up the emotional pressure of verbs or adjectives. Run your pen through each "very" (or search your computer file and highlight). Most things aren't very. "Absolutely," "purely," and the like are the same: most things aren't absolute or pure, and to claim so conveys a falsely emphatic tone. "Literally" is routinely misused, as when a Federal judge said that the Clinton administration was "literally and figuratively declaring war on the Special Prosecutor." The word means actually, in truth, in actual fact. Yet no tanks or cannons were drawn up around the Special Prosecutor's office. The judge meant, "Wow, I really feel this strongly!!" Screaming is not speaking well.

Keep your opinions pretty much to yourself. Strunk and White warn (p. 80) that "to air one's views gratuitously . . . is to imply that the demand for them is brisk." To air them intemperately reduces whatever demand there is. A comical example of what can go wrong with verbal abuse is: "These very tendentious arguments are false." The writer meant "tenuous" [look it up]. But even had she said "tenuous," the word "these" gives the reader the fleeting and hilarious impression that the writer was characterizing her own arguments, not the victim's. Tenuous and tendentious they are.

Wit compensates for tendentiousness, as in the literary careers of the journalist H. L. Mencken and the economist George Stigler. Mencken's railings against the boobocracy, or Stigler's against the bureaucracy, were made less tiresome by rhetorical coyness, ducking behind self-repudiating exaggeration or arch understatement. The reader allows such writers more room to be opinionated because their opinions are so amusingly expressed.

Most academic prose, from both students and faculty, could use more humor. There is nothing unscientific in self-deprecating jokes about the sample size, and nothing unscholarly in dry wit about the failings of intellectual opponents. Even a pun can bring cheer to a grader working through the 54th term paper. A writer must entertain if she is to be read. Only third-rate scholars and C students are so worried about the academic pose that they insist on their dignity. The Nobel laureate Robert Solow says of economic prose:

> Personality is eliminated from journal articles because it's felt to be "unscientific." An author is proposing a hypothesis, testing a hypothesis, proving a theorem, not persuading the reader that this is a better way of thinking about X than that. Writing would be better if more of us saw economics as a way of organizing thoughts and perceptions about economic life rather than as a poor imitation of physics. (1984)

14
Paragraphs Should
Have Points

So much for the essay as a whole. Turn then to the paragraph. (I'm not much enjoying the principle of arrangement I've imposed here: essay-paragraph-sentence-word. I wish I were better at such things.) The paragraph should be a more or less complete discussion of one topic. Paragraphing is punctuation, similar to stanzas in poetry. The stanzas can't be too long. You will want occasionally to pause for various reasons, having completed a bit of discussion, shifting the tone perhaps or simply giving the reader a break. The reader will skip around when her attention wanders, and will skip to the next paragraph. If your paragraphs are too long (as they will tend to be from a word processor, by the way) the reader will skip a lot of your stuff to get to the next break.

Paragraphs, though, should not be too short too often. The same is true of sentences.

Short paragraphs give a breathless quality to the writing.

Newspaper writers, especially on the sports page, often write in one-sentence paragraphs, for the sheer excitement of it.

Big quotations (in a block if more than four typed lines, always indented, *with no quotation marks* around the whole) have two legitimate jobs. First, they can give the devil his due. If you plan to rip to pieces a particular argument then you should quote it in full, to give at least the impression of being fair. Mild criticism, however, can't follow a big quote: you must indeed rip it to pieces, word by word. Otherwise the reader feels that the effort of settling into a new style has not been worthwhile. Second, block quotations can give an angel her voice. If the great economist Armen Alchian said something strikingly well with which you entirely agree, then you do not hurt your case by repeating what he said, and gaining from his greatness. Routine explanations do not belong anywhere, whether in long or short quotations. They convey the impression that you think with your scissors, and not very well.

A word is in order here about plagiarism. "Plagiarism" is using other people's turns of phrase with the intent of claiming them as your own. Please don't: it's childish and immoral. The worst students sometimes do it out of desperation, then claim that they didn't understand the rules. Because they are the worst students they often get caught. It's a serious offense, and in a well-run college results in expulsion. No college paper can be fashioned by stringing together passages from other writers. Your teachers know you can read, at least in the sense of spelling out the words. They want you to learn how to think and write. Please help them do it.

15
Make Tables, Graphs, and Displayed Equations Readable

The wretched tables and graphs in economics show how little economists care about expression. Tables and graphs are writing, and the usual rules of writing therefore apply. Bear your audience in mind. Try to be clear. Be brief. Ask: "Is this entry necessary? Would I dribble on in a similar way in prose or mathematics?" No reader wants the annual figures of income between 1900 and 1980 when the issue is the growth of income over the whole span. The reader wants statistics given in the simplest form consistent with their use. The eight digits generated by the average calculator are not ordinarily of any use. Who wants to read 3.14159256 when $3^1/_7$ describes the elasticity without making the reader stop to grasp the stream of numbers? (The point is widely misunderstood. Read Oskar Morgenstern, *On the Accuracy of Economic Observations*, 2nd ed., chapter 1.)

Titles and headings in tables should be as close to self-explanatory as possible. In headings of tables you should use words, not computer acronyms. Remember: you're trying to be clear, not Phony Scientific. A column labeled "LPDOM" requires a step of translation to get to the meaning: "Logarithm of the Domestic Price." You want people to understand your stuff, not to jump through mental hoops.

The same principles should guide graphs and diagrams. Edward R. Tufte's amazing book, *The Visual Display of Quantitative Information* (1983), demonstrates such precepts as "Mobilize every graphical element, perhaps several times over, to show the data" (p. 139; Tufte is not to be taken as a guide to writing prose). Everyone who uses tables or graphs should buy and study Tufte's book, and then reward themselves by getting his second book, *Envisioning Information* (1990). Use titles for diagrams and for tables that state their theme, such as "All Conferences Should Happen in the Midwest" instead of "A Model of Transport Costs." Use meaningful, spelled-out names for lines, points, and areas, not alphanumeric monstrosities: "Rich Budget Line" instead of "Locus QuERtY." You'll find it easier to follow your own argument and will be less likely to produce graphical nonsense.

The same things can be said of displayed equations. It's clearer and no less scientific to say "the regression was Quantity of Grain = 3.56 + 5.6 (Price of Grain) – 3.8 (Real Income)" than "the regression was $Q = 3.56 + 5.6P – 3.8Y$, where Q is quantity of grain, P its price, and Y real income." Anyone can retrieve the algebra from the words, but the reverse is pointlessly harder. The retrieval is hard even for professional mathematicians. The set theorist Paul Halmos said: "The author had to code his thought in [symbols] (*I deny that anybody thinks in [such] terms*), and the reader has to decode" (p. 38, italics mine). Stanislav Ulam, with many other mathematicians, complains of the raising of the symbolic ante: "I am turned off when I see only formulas and symbols, and little text. It is too laborious for me to look at such pages not knowing what to concentrate on" (1976, p. 275f). Tables, graphs, diagrams, and displayed equations should elucidate the argument, not obscure it.

16
Footnotes Are Nests for Pedants

A footnote should be subordinate. That is why it is at the foot. In academic and student writing, however, the most important work sometimes gets done in the small print at the bottom of the page. The worst sustained example in economics is Schumpeter's *History of Economic Analysis* (1954), in which the liveliest prose and the strongest points occur toward the end of footnotes spilling over three pages. Footnotes should not be used as a substitute for good arrangement. If the idea doesn't fit maybe it doesn't belong. Cluttering the main text with little side trips will break up the flow of ideas, like the footnote[1] attached to this sentence.

Footnotes should guide the reader to the sources. That's all. When they strain to do something else they get into trouble. Your attempt to assume the mantle of The Scholar looks foolish when the best you can do is cite the textbook. Citing whole books and articles is a disease in modern economics, spread by the author-date citation, such as that used in this book. It is easier for the author to write

---

[1] Inviting the reader to look away is not wise. Practically never is it a good idea to do what this note does, breaking a sentence. It should have been woven into the text, if it said anything, which it does not. Aren't you annoyed that I made you look down? Waste of time, yes? An amusing footnote on the matter, viewing it more cheerfully, is G. W. Bowersock, "The Art of the Footnote" (1983/84).

"See *The General Theory*" than to bother to find the page and sentence where Keynes, fatally, adopts the mistaken assumption of a closed economy. By not bothering to find it the author misses the chance to reread, and think.

<u>17</u>
Make Your Writing Cohere

Behind rules on what to avoid lies a rule on what to seek. It's the Rule of Coherence: make writing hang together. The reader can understand writing that hangs together, from phrases up to entire books. She can't understand writing filled with irrelevancies.

Look again at the paragraph I just wrote. It's no masterpiece, but you probably grasped it without much effort. The reason you did is that each sentence is linked to the previous one. The first promises a "rule." The second names it, repeating the word "rule"; after the colon the next bit delivers on the promise of the name, using the word "writing" for the first of three times and the phrase "hang together" for the first of two. The sentence next tells why it is a good rule, reusing "hang together" and introducing a character called "the reader," saying that she "can understand" certain writing. The final sentence emphasizes the point by putting it the other way, saying what writing she cannot understand. The paragraph itself hangs together and is easily grasped by the mind.

Economists would call it "transitive" writing. To do it you must violate the schoolmarm's rule of not repeating words. Verily, you *must* repeat them, linking the sentences and using pronouns like "it" or "them" to relieve monotony. The linkages can be tied neatly, if not too often, by repeating words with the same root in different versions, as was just done with the verb "linking" in the previous sentence and the noun "linkages" in this (the figure is called in classical rhetoric "polyptoton"). There are other tricks of cohesion. They rely on repetition. (In this paragraph for instance the word "repetition" is repeated right to the end in various forms: repetition, repeating, repeat, repeating, repetition.)

If you draw on the tricks you will be less likely to fill your prose with irrelevancies: (AB)(BC)(CD) looks pretty, is easy to understand, and is probably reasonable; (ABZYX)(MNOP)(BJKLC) looks ugly, is impossible to understand, and is probably nonsense. A newspaper editor once gave this advice to a cub reporter: "It doesn't much matter what your first sentence is. It doesn't even much matter what the second is. But the third damn well better follow from the first and second." If you once start a way of talking—a metaphor of birth in economic development or a tone of patient explanation to an idiot—you have to carry it through, making the third sentence follow from the others. You must reread what you have written again and again, unifying the tenses of the verbs, unifying the vocabulary, unifying the form. That's how to get unified, transitive paragraphs.

Yet, a clumsy way to get transitive paragraphs begins each sentence with a linking word. Indeed, not only did good Latin prose in the age of Cicero have this feature, but also Greek had it, even in common speech. In English, however, it is not successful. Therefore, many Ciceronian and Greek adverbs and conjunctions are untranslatable. To be sure, the impulse to coherence is commendable. But on the other hand (as must be getting clear by now), you tire of being pushed around by the writer, told when you are to take a sentence illustratively ("indeed"), adversatively ("yet," "however," "but"), sequentially ("furthermore," "therefore"), or concessively ("to be sure"). You are crushed by clanking machinery such as the hideous "not only... but also." English achieves coherence by repetition, not by signal. Repeat, and your paragraphs will cohere.

18
Use Your Ear

Prose has rhythms, some better than others. Abraham Lincoln and Martin Luther King knew rhythm in speech. Someone less gifted can at least avoid ugly rhythms by listening to what they have written. For instance, if every sentence is the same length and construction, the paragraph will become monotonous. If you have some dramatic reason for repeating the construction, the repetition is good. If you have no good reason for doing so, the reader will feel misled. If you talk always in sentences of precut form, the paragraph will have a monotonous rhythm. If you have been paying attention recently, you will see what I mean.

The novelist John Gardner gave some good advice about variety in sentences (p. 104f). Become self-conscious, he said, about how much you're putting into each part. An English sentence has grammatically speaking three parts: subject, verb, object. Thus: subject = "An English sentence"; verb = "has grammatically speaking" ("grammatically speaking" modifies the verb "has"); object = "three parts: subject, verb, object." Vary your sentences, Gardner suggested, by how much you put into each, and in each sentence choose only one of the three parts for elaboration. In the sentence just finished the score is: subject absent but understood = "you"; verb = "vary," complexly modified by "how much you put into each" object = "your sentences," quite simple, though not as simple as the subject. Gardner, who wrote pretty well, uncovered beautifully with his simple principle of the three sentence parts which we have just discussed and could discuss more if it were a good idea, which it is not, because we've said enough already, the graceless rhythm that results from an overburdened sentence such as this one, in which every part has much too much in it, every phrase too much in the way of excessive adjectives and too many adverbs modifying its elements, which exhausts the reader, and confuses him. Notice that you stopped paying attention about half way through it. A sentence with too much in all three of its parts can ruin a paragraph. (That last follows Gardner's Rule: a complex subject ["A sentence with too much in all three of its parts"] connected to a simple verb ["can ruin"] and simple object ["a paragraph"].)

19
Write in Complete Sentences

Which leads to the sentence. That is not one. Such tricks should be attempted only occasionally, and only for a reason (here: a dramatic surprise, if corny). Write mainly in complete sentences. This isn't a matter of school grammar. It's a matter of not raising expectations that you don't fulfill. As a fluent speaker of English (or at least of your dialect), you know when a sentence is a sentence by asking whether it could stand as an isolated remark. Now the phrase "As a fluent speaker of English" could stand alone, but only as an answer to a question in a conversation. Socrates: "Tell me, Polus: how do you know what an English sentence is?" Polus: "As a fluent speaker of English." Ask if it could stand alone as an isolated remark. No, it can't. If someone came up to you on the street and said "As a fluent speaker of English," you would expect her to continue. If, continuing to stare at you fixedly with a maniacal smile, she did not, you would edge carefully away.

20
Avoid Elegant Variation

The first duty in writing a sentence is to make it clear. A way to make it clear is to use one word to mean one thing. Get your words and things lined up and keep them that way. The positive rule is Strunk and White's: "Express parallel ideas in parallel form." [An example is about to happen:] The negative rule is Fowler's: "Avoid Elegant Variation." The two ideas are parallel and are expressed in parallel form: "The positive rule is" leads the reader to expect "The negative rule is." One hears every day the pair "positive" and "negative." The reader gets what she expects. She can fit the little novelties into what she already knows.

Elegant Variation uses many words to mean one thing, with the result in the end that the reader, and even the writer, don't quite know what is being talked about. A paper on economic development used in two pages all these: "industrialization," "growing structural differentiation," "economic and social development," "social and economic development," "development," "economic growth," "growth," and "revolutionized means of production." With some effort you can see in context that they all meant about the same thing. The writer simply liked the sound of the differences and had studied elegance too young. A writer on economic history wrote about the "indifferent harvests of 1815 and calamitous volume deficiencies of 1816." It takes a while to see that both mean about the same thing, a pretty simple thing. Notice that Elegant Variation often comes draped in five-dollar words ("growing structural differentiation" = new jobs in manufacturing; "indifferent harvests" = bad crops; "calamitous volume deficiencies" = very bad crops).

Some people who write this way mistake the purpose of writing, believing it to be a chance for empty display. The eighth grade, they should realize, is over. Most people do it out of correctable ignorance, as in: "the new economic history is concerned not only with what happened but also with why events turned out as they did." Something is wrong. The logic is that the reader imagines fleetingly that "what happened" and the "events [that] turned out as they did" are different things. She must give thought to whether they are. Elegant Variation requires the pointless effort to see that calamitous volume deficiencies are the same thing as bad crops. It wastes the reader's attention on unimportant matters. If the reader's attention strays a little—and it is always straying, a lot—she will come away from the sentence without knowing what it said.

Yet you also want to avoid *pointless* repetition. "It is a place where work gets done. The new plan gets done by setting a new agenda." The two "gets done" are not quite the same, so it's confusing to use the same phrase. Yet, yet: don't vary your words just to please Miss Jones.

21
Watch How Each Word
Connects with Others

Trimming away the elegant variation, like other rules of rewriting, does not make the writer's life easy. Most people's first drafts (including mine, believe me) are jammed with elegant variation, traffic signals, illogical sentences, nonsentences, misquotations, boilerplate, monotonies, and jingles. Easy writing, remember, makes hard reading. Dr. Johnson said two centuries ago, "What is written without effort is in general read without pleasure." Like effort in any work, such as sewing or auto repair, you must check and tighten, check and tighten. In short sessions the exercise will please you. It's good to do something well. The neat seam in a dress or the smooth joint in a fender revive the spirit worn from the effort. Still, before the end it is tiring. Do nouns and verbs link successive sentences? Have I used one word to mean one thing? Have I used parallel forms to emphasize parallel ideas? Can I drop any word? Check and tighten. The care extends to tiny details. For instance, you must choose repeatedly whether to carry over words from one construction to its parallel. Should you write "the beautiful and damned" or "the beautiful and *the* damned"?

Realize that in English gerunds ("supplying") and infinitives ("to supply") are close substitutes. You can say "Supplying a profitable forecast is a contradiction of economics" or "To supply a profitable forecast is a contradiction of economics." You can use the substitute to avoid a repetition that would otherwise be ugly or misleading, or to keep a parallelism.

Put modifiers—adjectives, adverbs, and whole phrases called in Miss Jones' class "participles"—close to the word they modify. Otherwise they tend to connect with other words and spoil the meaning.

Other tools to line up word and thing are singulars and plurals, masculines and feminines. Unlike the inflected Latin and Anglo-Saxon from which it descends, English does not have cases and gender (surviving in he, she, it, her, him, his, hers, its, I, me) to keep related words hitched. Use the few resources we have. The following sentence, for example, is ambiguous because "them" can refer to so many things: "*Owners* of the original and indestructible powers of the soil earned from *them* [powers or owners?] pure rents, and that tenant farmers were willing to pay *them* [the rents? the owners? the powers?] indicates that these powers of the soil were useful." You can work out what it means, but remember that the object is not to write so that the reader can understand but so that she cannot possibly misunderstand.

The singulars and plurals here are not essential to the meaning, and so they can be exploited to make it clear: "*An owner* of the original and indestructible powers of the soil earned from *them* [now effortlessly unambiguous because it agrees with the only plural referent available: the powers] pure rents, and that the tenant farmers were willing to pay *him* [unambiguous: the owner] indicates that these powers of the soil were useful." The use of "she" alongside "he" can in like fashion become an advantage for clarity of reference as much as a blow for sexual equality. If you assign gender to the two people you are talking about (as I do sometimes here in distinguishing the writer from the reader) then your reader will see what you mean.

Capitals are useful word-changes, too: you can make a word into a concrete and Proper Noun by capitalizing it, which is useful for reference. It's easy to point at a named Thing. That's why arguments in economics go by names, even by names of people: "the Coase Theorem" is more vivid than "the proposition that property rights matter to allocation in the case of high transaction costs" (which, incidentally, is the correct statement of the theorem, widely misunderstood in economics). Capitalization can be used nicely for referring to a Point in a diagram. Be careful, though: capitals have an Ironic Air to them, which is Fun only in Moderation (I tend to use them Too Much).

22
Watch Punctuation

Another detail is punctuation. You might think it would be easy, since there are only seven marks (excepting parentheses [and brackets, which are used in math style for parentheses within parentheses or for your insertions into someone else's words]). But feelings run strong on the matter. You should understand the old printer's conventions about spaces in typing after marks of punctuation. After a comma (,), semicolon (;), or colon (:), put one space before you start something new. After a period (.), question mark (?), or exclamation point (!), put two spaces. Just do it: don't argue. It makes word processing short of desk-top publishing look better.

You should also understand, and forgive, the strange convention about quotation marks and punctuation. Contrary to what you would think, "the close quote goes *inside* the mark of punctuation, thus." Look where the period is at the end of that last sentence. In the author-date system used in this book and in most of economics look at: "how one treats a quotation" (McCloskey 2000). Notice where the end quotation mark, the parentheses containing the citation, and the period are placed. You'll look silly if you do what freshmen do: "a quotation here followed by the close quotation mark and a period and then the lonely citation". (McCloskey 2000) Not evil: we're not talking child murder here, just picking up the wrong fork at a formal dinner. Don't do it.

The period is no problem, though to understand the most notable use of it in literature you have to know that in the English of England it is called a "full stop": in the last sentence of their spoof history of England, *1066 and All That*, Sellars and Yeatman write that after the First World War "America became Top Nation and history came to a." Nor is the question mark a problem: judge it by ear: are you using the questioning tone of voice? The dash—used like this, a sort of parenthesis spoken in a louder tone of voice—can be overused to solve a problem with a badly organized sentence (I do it a lot in drafts), but is not otherwise difficult.

A lot of people are confused about the colon (:) and the semicolon (;). The safest rule is that the colon indicates an illustration to follow: just like this. The semicolon indicates a parallel remark; it is (as here) an additional illustration. The semicolon (;) means roughly "furthermore"; the colon (:) means roughly "to be specific." The semicolon is also used to mark off items in series when the items themselves are long. "Faith, hope, and charity" uses commas; but if each item were elaborated ("Charity, the greatest of these, the light of the world"; and similarly with each) you might use the semicolon (;) as a sort of supercomma. You can see that the semicolon is also a sort of period lite; you can hurry the pace a bit by splicing two sentences with a semicolon, as here. So the semicolon falls between comma and period. Remember the difference between colon and semicolon by noting that the semicolon contains both a comma and a period within it, a printed compromise.

The comma. Here's where everyone gets confused or argumentative. Avoid the dreaded Comma Splice, I've just used one, I connected two sentences, now three, I intend to keep doing it, it will drive you crazy, it's a grade-school error, your boss will think you're a dope. The rule is if both clauses could stand alone as sentences then you need either a bigtime mark (period, semicolon, colon) or a conjunction. "The citizens lived in fear, the result was poor economic growth" contains a comma splice. Change it to: "The citizens lived in fear. The result was poor economic growth." or "The citizens lived in fear, and the result was poor economic growth." (And yet I have found comma splices in the writings of Matthew Arnold, admitted as one of the masters of English in the nineteenth century; it's social custom all the way down.)

Weak writers these days use too many commas, and use them by rule rather than by ear, probably because Miss Jones told them to. It's no rule of life, for instance, that "an if-clause always requires a comma after it" or "When a clause cannot stand alone it must be hedged with commas." In fact, such rules lead to a comma in nearly every sentence, and consequent slowing of pace. When applied too enthusiastically the rule-driven comma ends up separating subject from verb. (Notice that I *did* use a comma after the "In fact" in the sentence before last but *not* after "When applied too enthusiastically" in the next. Stay tuned.) In revision the trick is to delete most commas before "the," as I just did after "In revision," and did a couple of sentences earlier after "When applied too enthusiastically"; I didn't do it after "In fact" in the earlier sentence because the next word was not "the." The "the" signals a new phrase well enough without the clunk of a comma.

And yet: one must not be dogmatic about the comma. It is easy to fall into silly rules, mine as well as thine. The best rule is to punctuate by ear rather than by rule, and to insert a comma, as after "rule" here, where the pause in speaking seems to want it or where you as a reader get lost without it. When you want your prose to be read slowly and deliberately, and you have signaled this ponderous and academic tone in other ways as well, then use commas heavily. For most writing use them lightly.

23

The Order Around Switch Until It Good Sounds

Inflected languages have more freedom of order than English. In Latin *Homo canem mordet* means the same thing as *Canem mordet homo*, with only a difference of emphasis; but "man bites dog" and "dog bites man" are news items of different orders. Still, much can be done with the order of an English sentence. With the order of an English sentence much can be done. You can do much with the order of an English sentence. It's mainly a matter of ear: proper words in proper places. Tinker with the sentence until it works.

A problem comes with modifiers, especially with adverbs, which float freely in English. The phrase "which is *again merely* another notation for X" should be "which *again* is *merely* another notation for X." Moving the "again" prevents it from piling up against the other modifier. Or: "the elasticities are *both with respect* to the price" should be "both elasticities are with respect to the price." Until they work, try out the words in various places. In various places try out the words until they work. Try out the words in various places until they work. There. If you can't get them to work, give up the sentence as a bad idea.

You should cultivate the habit of mentally rearranging the order of words and phrases of every sentence you write. Rules, as usual, govern the rewriting. One rule of arrangement is to avoid breaking, as in this clause, the flow with parenthetical remarks. Put the remark at the end if it's important and at the beginning if it's not.

The most important rule of rearrangement is that the end of the sentence is the place of emphasis. I wrote the sentence first as "The end of the sentence is the emphatic *location*," which put the emphasis on the word "location." The reader leaves the sentence with the last word ringing in her ears. I wanted, however, to emphasize the idea of emphasis, not the idea of location. So I rewrote it as ". . . is the place of *emphasis*." You should examine every sentence to see whether the main idea comes at the end—or, second in emphasis, the beginning. Dump less important things in the middle, or in the trash. A corollary of the rule is that putting less important things at the end will weaken the sentence. It would be grammatical to write "That putting trivial things at the end will weaken the sentence *is a corollary of the rule*." Yet it shifts the emphasis to something already finished, *the rule*. The clearer way emphasizes the novelty, the idea of the weakened sentence, by putting it at the end.

Listen for sentences that are monotonously long or short; listen for straggling sentences, as in

That foolish young man of Japan,
Whose limericks never would scan.
When asked why it was
He replied, "It's because
I always try to get as much into the last line as I ever
    possibly can."

Adding one more idea at the last minute causes straggling, which comes even in a perfectly grammatical sentence like the present, making the sentence hard to read, which will cause the reader to stop reading after she has tried a couple of sentences like this one, which straggle, straggle, straggle. Remember Gardner's Rule of not complicating more than one of the triad subject, verb, object. The lengthy bits, as I said, should be at the end, although the rule will often conflict with the rule of putting the important matter at the end. At a minimum you should be aware of length and try it out in different portions of the sentence. The success of those eighth-grade ornaments, the doublet and the triplet (use them sparingly: write with a rifle, not a shotgun), depends critically on shifting the longest portions to the end: "Keynes and the Keynesians" works, "The Keynesians and Keynes" does not; "faith, hope, and charity" works, "charity, faith, and hope" does not.

24
Read, Out Loud

Reading out loud is a powerful technique of revision. By reading out loud you hear your writing as others hear it internally, and if your ear is good you'll detect the bad spots. For instance, it's practically impossible to decide when to use contractions like "you'll" or "it's" in semiformal prose without reading the sentence out loud. By reading out loud, furthermore, you'll pick up unintentional rhymes (at times your lines will chime), which can be distracting and mirth-provoking. Remember the rule: don't write anything that you would be embarrassed to read out loud to the intended audience. As usual, Hemingway had it right: "The writer needs a built-in, shockproof bullshit detector." You know more about good taste in the language, and how to spot bullshit, than you think. If in rereading your writing out loud you blush to hear an over-fancy sentence or a jargony word, change it.

No one, though, knows everything just because she's an English-speaking citizen. The ear is trained by exercise. Read the best old books (only when books are old do we know whether they *are* the best: the bestsellers of today are mostly rubbish). Take pleasure in the language of literature. Read poetry out loud, lots of it, the best. Memorize some of it (you know the lyrics of scores of rock songs: that's poetry; you might as well learn some of the real stuff, too). If you stop reading good writing when you leave school you will stop improving your ear. Even an economist's ear should ring with our English literature. Close study of *Time* and the *Wall Street Journal* doesn't normally suffice as an education in literacy—although it must be admitted that journalists like Meg Greenfield, Dave Barry, and P. J. O'Rourke use the newspaper language admirably well, and are good models. They got that way, though, by reading the real stuff, Shakespeare and Ring Lardner.

25
Use Verbs, Active Ones

Finally, words. The snappiest rules of good writing are about
words. For instance, write with nouns and, especially, verbs,
not with adjectives and adverbs. In revision the adjectives
and adverbs should be the first to go. Delete as many as you
can. Around 1830 the humorist Sydney Smith wrote, "In
composing, as a general rule, run your pen through every
other word you have written; you have no idea what vigour
it will give to your style." He might have followed his own
advice more fully, and would have done so if writing nowadays:

> ~~In composing~~ [*of course it's composing: that's what we're
> talking about, you dunce!*], ~~as a general rule~~ [*what would be
> the point of any other?*], run your pen through every other
> word ~~you have written~~ [*of course writing: again, that's what
> we're talking about; and in any case, what else would you run
> a pen through? Your finger?*]; you have no idea what vigour
> it will give ~~to your style~~ [*for goodness sake, how often do you
> have to repeat that you are talking about style?*]

The result is: "Run your pen through every other word; you
have no idea what vigour it will give." (In both Smith's version and mine the word "it" is ambiguous: it's not instantly
clear what "it" refers to. But that's another matter.)

Use active verbs: not "active verbs should be used,"
which is cowardice, hiding the user in the passive voice.
Rather: "you should use active verbs." The imperative is a
good substitute for the passive, especially for taking a reader

through mathematical arguments: "then divide both sides by x" instead of "both sides are then divided by x."

Verbs make English. If you pick out active, accurate, and lively verbs you will write in an active, accurate, and lively style. You should find the action in a sentence and express it in a verb. Expressing it in a phrase functioning as a noun saps vigor. The disease is called "nominalization," and it afflicts most academic prose (mine, for instance). The teacher of style, Joseph Williams, who discusses nominalization at length, gives an example that might have come from economics: "There is a data reanalysis need." The only verb is the colorless "is," and the real action is buried in the nouns "need" and "reanalysis" (Williams, p. 12). You can fix such a sentence by using verbs: "We must reanalyze our data." Circle every "is" in your writing, and if the page looks like a bad case of acne, replace every "is" with a real, action verb.

"There is" and "It is" often cause problems. (I wrote that first as "are often problems," then thought better and found the action in the sentence.) Notice that a real verb requires a real subject. There's no place to hide. The "data reanalysis need," by contrast, merely exists, blessedly free from personal responsibility (the freedom from responsibility makes nominalization popular among bureaucrats; that's us, often, so don't sneer). Find the actor and the action. Find the verb. You have no idea what vigor it will bring.

26
Avoid Words That Bad Writers Love

Because it's easy at the level of the single word to detect and punish crime the legislative attitude toward prose reaches its heaven in lists of Bad Words. Some perfectly good English words have died this way: for instance, "ain't." Good writers have mental lists of words to avoid. At a minimum certain words will tag you as incompetent simply because good writers have decided so. For example, though it's unfair to the inexperienced and there's nothing whatever in the nature of the linguistic universe to justify it, you might as well know that in some company if you use "hopefully" to mean "I hope" you will be set down as a fool. Hopefully General Booth entered heaven is supposed to mean "with hope," not "I hope."

If economic prose would drop "via," "the process of," "intra," "and/or," "hypothesize," "respectively," and (a strange one, this) "this" the gain in clarity and grace would be big. If it would drop "at least minimal," "process of," "thus," "overall," "basic," and "factor" the world would be saved. The best practice provides the standard. Virginia Woolf would not write "and/or" or "he/she" because she wanted prose, not a diagram. Some others that I'm sure Virginia would have disliked appear in my personal list of **Bad Words**.

Vague nouns and pronouns:

concept: a vague, Latinate (that is, pretentiously derived from Latin), front-parlor word; consider "idea," "notion," or "thought."

data: over- and mis-used in economics. "Data" are plural, although the word is clearly on its way to becoming singular in the language. "Data" means "givens" in Latin, and that is how you should use it, not as a do-all synonym for "facts," "statistics," "information," "observations," and so forth. The word embodies, incidentally, a dangerous attitude toward observation—that it is "given" by someone else—but the point here is one of style. "Datum" is one "data," though only pedants use it.

function: in the sense of "role" is Latinate.

situation: vague. "Position" or "condition" are better, depending on the meaning.

individuals: for plain "people."

agents: the same.

structure: vague. There are no obvious alternatives to structure because the word usually doesn't mean anything at all. On this and other similar words in economics, see Fritz Machlup (1963, 1967).

process: usually empty, and can be struck out (sometimes with its "the") without changing the meaning: "the economic development process" or "the transition process" become plain "economic development" or "the transition."

the existence of: strike it out, and just name the thing.

time frame: means "time"; it originates in the engineer's dim notion that "time" means "passage of time" alone, and not "a point in time" (another engineering expression). But the notion is false.

Pretentious and feeble verbs:

critique: elegant variation for "criticize" or "to read critically" or "to comment on."

implement: Washingtonese, a rich and foolish dialect of Economese.

comprise: fancy talk for "include" or "consist of."

analyze: over- and mis-used in economics as a synonym for "discuss" or "examine." Look it up in your dictionary. It meant in Greek "cut to pieces."

hypothesize: for "suppose" or "expect." This word tags you (similar words: "finalize," "and/or," "time frame").

finalize: boardroom talk. See "hypothesize," academic boardroom talk.

state: in the mere sense of "say"; why not say "say"? "State means "assert, with conviction."

try and do something is "try to do something" (strangely, "try and" is common among educated English people; in the United States it is a marker of incompetence).

the reason was due to: try again.

Pointless adjectives:

former... latter: the above; the preceding: and other words that request the reader to look back to sort out the former and latter things. Don't request the reader to look back, because she will, and will lose her place. Never ask the reader to solve a puzzle, because she won't be able to and will get angry.

aforementioned: what are you writing, a will?

intra/inter: do not use. Do not present verbal puzzles to your reader. Everyone has to stop to figure out what these prefixes mean. Use "within" and "between." "International" and "intramural" are fine, of course, being well domesticated. But "The inter- and intra-firm communication was weak" is silly. Fancy talk.

interesting: a weak word, made weak by its common sarcastic use and by its overuse by people with nothing to say about their subject except that it is interesting. It arouses the reader's sadism.

kind of, sort of, type of: vague, vague, vague. Use sparingly.

Useless adverbs:

fortunately, interestingly, etc.: cheap ways of introducing irrelevant opinion.

respectively: as in "Consumption and investment were 90% and 10% of income, respectively." Why would anyone reverse the correct order of the numbers? (Answer: someone who does not express parallel ideas in parallel form.) Drawing attention to the lack of parallelism by mentioning explicitly that it did *not* take place is a bad idea. When the list is longer, distribute the numbers directly; "Consumption was 85% of income, investment 10%, and government spending 5%."

very: the very general rule is to think very hard before using "very" very much, and to very often strike it out. It's a weak word.

for convenience: as in, "For convenience, we will adopt the following notation." A silly phrase, when you think about it. All writing should be for convenience. What would be the point of writing for inconvenience?

Often you'll find that adverbs can be dropped (look for words ending in -ly). They often convey your opinion, which only your mother cares about.

Clumsy conjunctions:

due to: usually signals a clumsy phrase, due to not arranging the sentence to sound right.

via: plain "by" is the word wanted.

in terms of: clumsy and vague; compare "due to."

thus and *hence:* use traffic signals sparingly.

plus to mean *and:* use "and" until the language has finished changing "plus" into "and," which will take another century or so. I know you use it when you talk. Well, speech can be improved by writing, too.

The vocabulary of economics, like other vocabularies, is enriched by coinages and borrowings: the Laffer curve, the affluent society, the agency problem. Contrary to a widespread impression among non-economists, though, mastering the vocabulary of economics is not the same as mastering economics.

Everyone, economist or not, comes equipped with a vocabulary for the economy. It might be called Ersatz Economics. In Ersatz Economics, prices start by "skyrocketing." When "sellers outnumber buyers" prices fall from "exorbitant" or "gouging" levels, down through "fair" and "just." If this "vicious cycle" goes on too long, though, they fall to "unfair" and "cutthroat," the result of "dumping." Likewise, the woman in the street believes she knows that unions and corporations have more "bargaining power" than do their victims, and therefore can "exploit" them. A consumer can "afford" medical care, maybe only "barely afford" it, "needs" housing, and views food as a "basic necessity." Business people maintain their "profit margins," probably "obscene" or "unwarranted," by "passing along" a higher wage, which causes workers to demand still higher wages, in a "spiral." The protection of the American worker's "living wage" from "unfair competition" by "cheap foreign labor" should be high on the nation's list of "priorities," as should be the "rebuilding" of our "collapsing" industrial "base."

To write thoughtfully in economics you must clear your mind of such cant, as to understand astronomy you must stop talking about the sun "rising."

27
Be Concrete

A good general rule of words is Be Concrete. A singular word is more concrete than a plural (compare "Singular words are more concrete than plurals"). Definiteness is concrete. Prefer Pepperidge Farm to bread, bread to widgets, and widgets to X. Bad writers in economics sometimes use abstraction because they have nothing to say and don't want the fact to become too plain, in the style of educational bureaucrats. Mostly, though, they use abstraction to get general. They don't believe that the ordinary reader will understand that "Pepperidge Farm" can stand for any commodity or that "ships" can stand for all capital. Secret codes use the principle that translation is often easier in one direction than the other. Contrary to what most economic writers seem to think, of course, a reader finds it harder to translate abstractions down into concrete examples than to translate examples up into abstract principles. Much economic writing reads like a code. "%& * marginal# #$$ processof& %$ #@ #$ % !structure."

Professional economists develop into professional code breakers. To an economist there does seem to be much wrong with a sentence such as this: "Had *capital and labor* in 1860 embodied the same *technology* used in 1780, the *increase in capital* would barely have offset the fixity of land." Here is a better way: "Had the *machines and men* of 1860 embodied the same *knowledge of how to spin cotton or move cargo* as in 1780, the *larger numbers of spindles and ships* would have barely offset the fixity of land." In a paper on Australia the phrase "sheep and wheat" would do just fine in place of "natural resource-oriented exports." In a paper on economic history "Spanish prices began to rise before the treasure came" would do just fine in place of "the commencement of the Spanish Price Revolution antedated the inflow of treasure." Writing should make things clear, not put them into a code of Latinate abstraction.

28
Be Plain

The encoding often uses five-dollar words to support a pose of The Scientist or The Scholar. The pose is pathetic: science and scholarship depend on the quality of argument, not on the level of diction. "The integrative consequences of growing structural differentiation" means in human-being talk "the need for others that someone feels when he buys rather than bakes his bread." Anglo-Saxon words (need, someone, feels, buys, bread, bake) have often acquired a concreteness through homely use that more recent and more scholarly coinages from Latin or Greek have not (integrative, consequences, structural, differentiation: all directly from Latin, without even a domesticating sojourn in French). "Geographical and cultural factors function to spatially confine growth to specific regions for long periods of time" means in Anglo-Saxon and Norman French "it's a good bet that once a place gets poor it will stay poor."

Five-dollar words sometimes are fun. In the hands of a master they transmit irony, as in the analysis of sports by the great American economist, Thorstein Veblen: sports "have the advantage that they afford a politely blameless outlet for energies that might otherwise not readily be diverted from some useful end." But you've got to be Veblen to get away with such stuff. In most hands it's just Latin-fed, polysyllabic baloney: "Thus, it is suggested, a deeper understanding of the conditions affecting the speed and ultimate extent of an innovation's diffusion is to be obtained only by explicitly analyzing the specific choice of technique problem which its advent would have presented to objectively dissimilar members of the relevant (historical) population of potential adopters." Come off it, Professor D.

A lot of economic jargon hides a five-cent thought in a five-dollar word. Economists have forgotten that it's jargon. "Current period responses" means "what people do now"; "complex lagged effects" means "the many things they do later." "Interim variation" means "change"; "monitored back" means "told." Economists would think more clearly if they recognized a simple thought for what it is. The "time inconsistency problem" is the economics of changing one's mind. The "principal/agent problem" is the economics of what hirelings do.

The great jargon-generating function in economics is what may be called the teutonism, such as der Grossjargongeneratingfunktion. German actually invents words like these, with native roots that no doubt make them evocative to German speakers (classical Sanskrit did it too, using as many as twenty elements). Again it does not suit the genius of modern English. A common one is "private wealth-seeking activity," which is a knot in the prose. Untie it: "the activity of seeking wealth privately." When laid out in this way, with the liberal use of "of," the phrase looks pretty flabby. "Private" is understood anyway, "Activity of" is pointless (note that nothing happens when you strike it out and reform the phrase). By the principle of untying the knot "the seeking of wealth" is what is left.

The unknotting will introduce "of" a lot: "factor price equalization" is muddy, though a strikingly successful bit of mud; "the equalization *of* the prices *of* factors" is clearer, if straggling. Most teutonisms do not make it as attempts to coin new jargon. "Elastic credit supply expectations rise" is

81

too much to ask of any reader: she must sort out which word goes with which, whether the supply or the expectations are elastic, and what is rising. Hyphens help, but impose more notation. The reader can digest "The long-run balance of payments adjustment" much easier if it's put as "the adjustment of the balance of payments in the long run." The result is inelegant, but no less elegant than the original, and clearer. Here are more knots that the reader must stop to untie: "anti-quantity theory evidence"; "contractually uniform transaction cost"; "initial relative capital goods price shock"; "any crude mass expulsion of labor by parliamentary enclosure thesis"; "community decision making process"; "Cobb-Douglas production function estimation approach"; "alternative property rights schemes."

The possessive, unless attached to a proper noun (Samuelson's genius, Gary's pride), is not used much by good writers. It's overused by poor writers, who delight in phrases like "the standard economist's model." The possessive is a teutonism generator and has the teutonic ambiguity: what's standard, the model or the economist? Sure, you can figure it out: but a writer is not supposed to leave a bunch of things for you to figure out.

Remember Sydney Smith running his pen through every other word: You should reexamine any phrase with more than one adjective, considering whether it might be best in leaner form, and should watch especially for nouns used as adjectives. It *is* the genius of English to let verbs become nouns and nouns adjectives. You go to the club, get a go in cribbage, and hear that all systems are go at the Cape. What is objectionable is piling up these nounverbadjectives teutonically.

29
Avoid Cheap Typographical Tricks

Another objectionable practice is the acronym, such as "Modigliani and Miller (henceforth M&M)" or "purchasing power parity (PPP)." Besides introducing zany associations with candy and second-grade humor, the practice pimples the page and adds a burden of excess notation on the reader. The demands of the computer have worsened the situation. Resist, and remember that even expert mathematicians do not think in symbols. An occasional GDP or CAB won't hurt anyone, but even such a commonplace as GDCF pains all but the most hardened accountant. "Gross domestic capital formation" is fine once or twice to fix ideas, but then "capital formation" or (after all) plain "it" will do the job. Believe me: people will not keep slipping into thinking of it as NDCF or GCF or GC. The point is to be clear, not to "save space" (as the absurd justification for acronyms has it, absurd because the acronyms in most long papers save a half dozen lines of print, less than the pointless table-of-contents paragraph). As usual, good writers set the standard of what to do. You won't find them baffling their readers with LQWAGE and BBLUUBB.

Certain other typographical devices need careful handling. Use these "devices" sparingly, they add an "air" of (henceforth "AAO") Breathlessness or Solemnity or *Coyness*! The *point* is that they *add* something, *instead* of "letting it speak for *itself*" (LISFI). They are, so to speak, *sound effects*! The *reader* "understands" this, and doubts *everything* that is said!! LISFI is better. Using these "devices" instead of LISFI suggests that something is wrong with the prose as is. If you use *italics* (underlining) to make your point clear it is probably because the *sentence* is badly set up to give emphasis *naturally.* Fix it. If you use "quotation marks" all the time when not actually "quoting" someone, it is probable that you wish to "apologize" for the "wrong" word or to sneer at "it." Don't. It's impolite to cringe or to sneer.

Don't justify (align the right margin in) an essay meant for an academic audience. That is, set your computer to produce a ragged right margin. The rule is a good example of the arbitrary, picking-up-the-right-fork character of some rules. Justification makes it look like you value cute tricks with your computer more than the writing itself. And it often   produces   lines   like   this   one.

30
Avoid This, That, These, Those

Another plague is this-ism. These bad writers think this reader needs repeated reminders that it is *this* idea, not *that* one, which is being discussed. Circle the "this" and "these" in your draft: you'll be surprised at their number. The "this" points the reader back to the thing referred to, for no good reason. No writer wants her reader to look back, for looking back is looking away, interrupting the forward flow and leaving the reader looking for her place. Thises and thats are demonstrative pronouns on the way to becoming the definite article ("le" and la" in French come from Latin "ille" and "illa" = "that"; ancient Greek went through a similar development from Homeric to Attic). But we already have a definite article. It's called "the" (derived from an Indo-European word meaning "that"). Often the plain "the" will do fine, and keep the reader reading. Consider repeating the word represented by "this." Repetition, remember, brings clarity and unity to English. The rule is to query every "this" or "these." Take most of them out.

31
Above All, Look at Your Words

Beyond such matters of taste lies idiom. You must write English, no easy matter. The prepositions of English are its substitute for the grammatical cases that inflected languages have. Prepositions cause trouble. Try experimenting to get them right: is it "by" an increase "of" supply or "because" of an increase "in" supply? God and the best writers know. Verbs often come preposition-enriched: write down, write up, and the like. Pare the prepositions away if they are not essential.

Words often come in pairs: one "overcomes," not "cures," one's ignorance. Thinking in word pairs, on the other hand, leads to the cliché. Flee the cliché when a more original word is precise and vivid. Observe what varied thoughts about "the pursuit of profit" are suggested by fleeing the cliché: seeking or finding or having or uncovering or coming upon or bumping into profit; and pursuing gain or maximum wealth or opportunities or stimuli or satisfaction or success. The Austrian economist F. A. Hayek said that he came to understand the role of information in a market economy by thinking hard about a phrase his colleagues at the London School of Economics in the 1930s found merely funny: the ignorant redundancy "given data" (as I've noted, the word "data" already means "givens," in Latin). "That led me, in part, to ask to whom were the data really given. To us [staff at the school], it was of course to nobody. . . . That's what led me, in the thirties, to the idea that the whole problem was the utilization of information dispersed among thousands of people and not possessed by anyone." New words imply new thoughts. Wordthought is a part of thinking.

One should think what a word literally means and what it connotes. English is jammed with dead metaphors, easily brought to life with incongruous effect. Good writers examine their words for literal meaning, to make sure that the metaphors remain dead or are at the least brought to life in a decorous way. Look at what you have written: are the words literally possible? "The indicators influenced the controls." How does an indicator influence a control? Someone wrote "the severity of the models." Punishments, not models, can be "severe." What he meant is that the models make assumptions that are hard to believe. He should have found words to say it: unbelievability, implausibility.

There is no end to word lore. Study of dictionaries and style books and the best writing of the ages will make you at least embarrassed to be ignorant, the beginning of wisdom. You should know that "however" works better in a secondary position. You should know that "in this period" is usually redundant, that numbered lists are clumsy (so I have used one to arrange my book!), that "not only . . . but also" is a callow Latinism, that "due to" is bureaucratese, that use of "regarding X" or "in regard to X" is definite evidence of a bad education in the language.

Be of good cheer. You have plenty of company in such errors. We all have a lot to learn.

If You Didn't Stop Reading, Join the Flow

Good style is above all a matter of taste. Professional economists share with college sophomores, I noted at the outset, the conviction that matters of taste are "mere matters of opinion," the notion being that "opinion" is unarguable. A matter of taste, however, can be argued, often to a conclusion. The best argument is social practice, since that is what taste is. Many people with a claim to know have listed the same rules for writing English, which fact is itself a powerful argument. Mark Twain listed seven rules, familiar now, which would revolutionize economics. The writer must:

1. *Say* what he is proposing to say, not merely come near it.
2. Use the right word, not its second cousin.
3. Eschew surplusage.
4. Not omit necessary details.
5. Avoid slovenliness of form.
6. Use good grammar.
7. Employ a simple and straightforward style.

George Orwell, fifty years later, narrowed the rules down to six:

1. Never use a metaphor, simile or other figure of speech which you are used to seeing in print.
2. Never use a long word where a short one will do.
3. If it is possible to cut a word out, always cut it out.

4. Never use the passive where you can use the active.
5. Never use a foreign phrase, a scientific word, or a jargon word if you can think of an everyday English equivalent.
6. Break any of these rules sooner than say anything outright barbarous.

To improve in writing style you must become your own harshest editor and grader, as you must become your harshest coach to improve in running or your harshest critic to improve in thinking generally. Good writing is difficult. Economics, however, is too fine a subject to be left in a verbal mess out of mere laziness. What is at first difficult becomes a pleasure in the end, like any skill of civilization, an occasion for flow.

In brief, then: We can do better, much better, than the say-what-you're-going-to-say, elegant variation, inefficient exposition, boilerplate, incoherent paragraphs, impenetrable tables, unemphatic word order, straggling sentences, contrived triplets, verbosity, nominalization, passive verbs, barbaric neologisms, abstractions, five-dollar words, teutonisms, acronyms, this-es, and fractured idioms of modern economic prose. Please. For our splendid science.

Works Cited

Bartlett, John. 1955. *Familiar Quotations*, 13th ed. Boston: Little, Brown.

Barzun, Jacques. 1976. *Simple and Direct: A Rhetoric for Writers*. New York: Harper and Row.

Barzun, Jacques, and Henry F. Graff. 1970. *The Modern Researcher*. New York: Harcourt Brace.

Becker, Howard S. 1986. *Writing for Social Scientists: How to Start and Finish Your Thesis, Book, or Article*. Chicago: University of Chicago Press.

Booth, Wayne C. 1974. *Modern Dogma and the Rhetoric of Assent*. Chicago: University of Chicago Press.

Bowersock, Glen W. 1983/1984. "The Art of the Footnote." *The American Scholar* 53: 54–63.

Cohen, J. M., and M. J. Cohen. *The Penguin Dictionary of Modern Quotations*, 2nd ed. Harmondsworth, Middlesex: Penguin.

Csikszentmihalyi, Mihaly. 1997. *Finding Flow: The Psychology of Engagement with Everyday Life*. New York: Basic.

Dillard, Annie. 1989. *The Writing Life*. New York: Harper.

Fowler, H. W. 1926 (1965). *Modern English Usage*. Oxford: Oxford University Press.

Galbraith, J. K. 1978. "Writing, Typing and Economics." *Atlantic* 241 (March): 102–105.

Gardner, John. 1983. *The Art of Fiction: Notes on Craft for Young Writers*. New York: Knopf.

Gowers, Sir Ernest. 1962. *The Complete Plain Words*. London: Penguin.

Graves, Robert, and Alan Hodge. 1943 (1961). *The Reader Over Your Shoulder: A Handbook for Writers of English Prose*. New York: Macmillan.

Hall, Donald. 1979. *Writing Well*, 3rd ed. Boston: Little, Brown.

Halmos, Paul R. 1973. In Steenrod, Norman E. and others, *How to Write Mathematics*, pp. 19–48. No city: American Mathematics Society.

James, Simon. 1984. *A Dictionary of Economic Quotations*. Totowa, NJ: Barnes and Noble.

Lanham, Richard A. 1987. *Revising Prose*, 2nd ed. New York: Macmillan.

Lewis, Norman. 1983. *A Dictionary of Correct Spelling: A Handy Reference Guide*. New York: Barnes and Noble.

Lucas, F. L. 1955 (1974). *Style*. London: Cassell.

Machlup, Fritz. 1963 (1967). *Essays in Economic Semantics*. New York: Norton.

McCloskey, Deirdre. 1985. "Economical Writing." *Economic Inquiry* 24 (April): 187–222.

McCloskey, Deirdre. 1997. *The Vices of Economists; The Virtues of the Bourgeoisie*. Ann Arbor and Amsterdam: University of Michigan and University of Amsterdam Press.

McCloskey, Deirdre. 1998. *The Rhetoric of Economics*. 2nd revised ed. Madison: University of Wisconsin Press.

McCloskey, Deirdre, and Stephen Ziliak. 1996. "The Standard Error of Regression." *Journal of Economic Literature* 34 (March): 97–114.

Medawar, Peter. "Is the Scientific Paper Fraudulent?" *Saturday Review* 47 (August 1): 42–43.

Mills, C. Wright. 1959. "On Intellectual Craftsmanship." In his *The Sociological Imagination*. New York: Grove.

Morgenstern, Oskar. 1963. *On the Accuracy of Economic Observations*, 2nd ed. Princeton: Princeton University Press.

Oakeshott, Michael. 1933. "Poetry as a Voice in the Conversation of Mankind," in his *Experience and Its Modes*.

Reprinted in *Rationalism in Politics*. 1962. New York: Basic Books.

Orwell, George. 1946. "Politics and the English Language." Reprinted in Sonia Orwell and Ian Angus, eds. 1968. *The Collected Essays, Journalism and Letters of George Orwell*, Vol. IV, *In Front of Your Nose*, 1945–1950. New York: Harcourt Brace Jovanovich.

Oxford Dictionary of Quotations, 2nd ed. 1953. London: Oxford University Press.

Piaget, Jean, and Jean-Claude Bringuier. 1980. *Conversations with Jean Piaget*. Chicago: University of Chicago Press.

Popper, Karl. 1976. *Unended Quest: An Intellectual Autobiography.* Glasgow: Collins.

Quintilian. 1980. *Institutio Oratoria*. Cambridge: Harvard University Press.

Salant, Walter. 1969. "Writing and Reading in Economics." *Journal of Political Economy* 77 (July/August): 545–558.

Solow, Robert. 1984. Letter of February 27 to McCloskey.

Strunk, William, Jr., and E. B. White. 1979. *The Elements of Style,* 3rd ed. New York: Macmillan.

Tufte, Edward R. 1983. *The Visual Display of Quantitative Information*. Cheshire, CT: Graphics Press.

Twain, Mark. 1895. "Fenimore Cooper's Literary Offenses." *The North American Review* (July). Reprinted in *The Unabridged Mark Twain*. 1976. Philadelphia: Running Press.

Ulam, Stanislaw. 1976. *Adventures of a Mathematician*. New York: Scribner's.

Webster's New World Dictionary of the American Language, 2nd college ed. 1976. Cleveland: William Collins & World.

Williams, Joseph M. 1981. *Style: Ten Lessons in Clarity and Grace*. Glenview, IL: Scott, Foresman.

Williamson, Samuel T. 1947. "How to Write Like a Social Scientist." *Saturday Review* 20 (October): 17 ff.

Index